Alice Cooper
Wolfgang »Bubi« Heilemann

Alice Cooper

LIVE ON TOUR – BACKSTAGE – PRIVATE
PHOTOS 1973–1975

Photos: Wolfgang »Bubi« Heilemann

Text: Bubi Heilemann & Sabine Thomas

SCHWARZKOPF & SCHWARZKOPF

INHALT

Steckbrief	9
Alice Cooper: Der Schock-Rocker	10
Eine Schlange namens Yvonne	34
Live in the USA: Die Billion-Dollar-Babies-Tour	42
On tour mit Alice, Uschi und Dalí	62
Alices rockige Horror-Show in Deutschland	78
»Hi, this is Alice Cooper speaking!«	116
Update	132
Information & Danksagungen	134
Edition Bubi Heilemann	135

CONTENTS

Biography	9
Alice Cooper: Shock rocker	11
A snake called Yvonne	35
Live in the USA: The Billion Dollar Babies tour	43
On tour with Alice, Uschi and Dalí	63
Alice's rocky horror show in Germany	79
»Hi, this is Alice Cooper speaking!«	117
Update	133
Information & Acknowledgements	134
Bubi Heilemann series	135

»Welcome To My Nightmare«

(ALICE COOPER)

STECKBRIEF / BIOGRAPHY
ALICE COOPER

Name: Vincent Damon Furnier
Geburtsdatum: 4. Februar 1948
Geburtsort: Detroit/Michigan (USA)
Eltern: Ether Moroni Furnier (Prediger), Ella Furnier
Geschwister: Schwester Nickie
Familienstand: Verheiratet mit der Tänzerin Sheryl Goddard (seit 1976)
Kinder: Calico Zane (*1981), Dashiell Vincent (*1984), Sonora Rose (*1993)
Hobbys: Fernsehen, Golf spielen, Autos und Uhren sammeln
Werdegang: Nach der Schulzeit an der Cortez High School in Arizona besuchte Vincent Damon Furnier die Kunstakademie und studierte Malerei. Sein großes Vorbild war der spanische Surrealist Salvador Dalí, der sich Jahre später als Alice-Cooper-Fan outen sollte ... Auf der High School freundete er sich mit Gitarrist Glen Buxton und Bassist Dennis Dunaway an, mit denen er 1964 seine erste Band The Earwigs (dt.: Ohrwürmer) gründete, die später unter den Namen The Spider und The Nazz ein paar Singles veröffentlichte.

1968 benannten sich Vince und seine Freunde in die Alice Cooper Band um. Wie es zu diesem Namen kam, darüber existieren verschiedene Versionen: Angeblich spielte die Band im Hause ihres damaligen Managers mit einem Ouija Board, und der Geist, der aus dem Jenseits mit ihnen Kontakt aufnahm, hieß Alice Cooper. Jahrelang hielt sich auch hartnäckig das Gerücht, dass Vince die Reinkarnation einer Hexe namens Alice Cooper sei, die im düsteren Mittelalter auf dem Scheiterhaufen verbrannt wurde. Vince (der seinen Namen später offiziell in Alice Cooper ändern ließ) erzählte mir bei unserer ersten Begegnung, dass er einfach das Telefonbuch von L.A. aufgeschlagen und mit geschlossenen Augen auf einen Namen getippt hat: Alice Cooper.

Die Band versuchte ihr Glück zunächst in Los Angeles. Frank Zappa bezeichnete sie als »schlechteste Band von L.A.« und nahm sie trotzdem – oder gerade deswegen – sofort für sein Label Straight Records unter Vertrag. 1969 erschien das erste Album von Alice Cooper mit dem Titel »Pretties For You«, 1970 folgte die LP »Easy Action«. Beide Alben floppten. Die Band siedelte um nach Detroit und nahm dort unter den Fittichen von Produzent Bob Ezrin 1971 ihr drittes Album »Love It To Death« auf. In den Staaten und in Großbritannien stürmten die LP und die daraus ausgekoppelte Single »I'm Eighteen« die Charts. Ende 1971 folgte das Album »Killer«. Mit dem 1972 veröffentlichten Album »School's Out« und dem gleichnamigen Titel-Track gelang Alice Cooper der internationale Durchbruch.

ALICE COOPER BAND:
Vincent Damon Furnier alias Alice Cooper (voc)
Glen Buxton (git)
Dennis Dunaway (b)
Michael Bruce (git / kb)
Neal Smith (dr)

Name: Vincent Damon Furnier
Date of birth: 4 February 1948
Place of birth: Detroit/Michigan (USA)
Parents: Ether Moroni Furnier (preacher), Ella Furnier
Siblings: One sister (Nickie)
Marital status: Married to dancer Sheryl Goddard (since 1976)
Children: Calico Zane (*1981), Dashiell Vincent (*1984), Sonora Rose (*1993)
Hobbies: Watching television, playing golf, collecting cars and watches
Career: After graduating from Cortez High School in Arizona, Vincent Damon Furnier enrolled at Glendale Community College to major in art, although he later dropped out. One of his main influences was the Spanish surrealist Salvador Dalí, who years later revealed that he in turn was a fan of Alice Cooper. While still at high school Vince had become friends with guitarist Glen Buxton and bassist Dennis Dunaway. In March 1964 they formed their first group, The Earwigs, who later released a few singles under the names The Spiders and The Nazz.

In 1968 the group changed its name to Alice Cooper. For years, various tales persisted about how they had arrived at their name. According to one story, some of the band were experimenting with a Ouija board in their manager's house and Alice Cooper was the name of a spirit in the room. For years rumour also had it that Vince was the reincarnation of a girl named Alice Cooper, who had been burnt at the stake as a witch in the Middle Ages. Vince (who later legally changed his name to Alice Cooper) also told me when we first met that he'd simply opened the Los Angeles telephone directory and with his eyes shut pointed to a name at random.

The band first tried its luck in Los Angeles. Frank Zappa called them »the worst band in LA,« but still – or maybe because of that – quickly signed them to his Straight Records label. In 1969 Alice Cooper's debut album »Pretties For You« was released, followed in 1970 by »Easy Action,« but both records bombed. The band then moved to Detroit, where in early 1971 they recorded their third album, »Love It To Death,« under the tutelage of fledgling producer Bob Ezrin. The single »I'm Eighteen« reached the top of the US charts. The follow-up album, »Killer,« was released later that year, but the group's international breakthrough only came in 1972 with the release of the album and single »School's Out.«

ALICE COOPER BAND:
Vincent Damon Furnier alias Alice Cooper (vocals)
Glen Buxton (guitar)
Dennis Dunaway (bass)
Michael Bruce (guitars & keyboards)
Neal Smith (drums)

ALICE COOPER: DER SCHOCK-ROCKER

Sommer '72: Alice Cooper veröffentlichte rechtzeitig zum Ferienbeginn das Album »School's Out« und stürmt damit weltweit die Charts. Millionen Teenies auf der ganzen Welt grölten am letzten Schultag aus vollem Hals: »Schooooool's out for summer! Schooooool's out for-ever!« Eine Hymne war geboren.

Im Oktober 1972 schwappten die ersten Warnungen aus den USA zu uns herüber: »Vorsicht – der Rockteufel kommt! Wer hat Angst vor Alice? Wer zittert mit?«

14. November 1972, Circus Krone in München: Das Konzert war bereits seit Wochen ausverkauft, auf dem Schwarzmarkt erreichten die Tickets astronomische Preise. Seit über einer Stunde drängten sich rund 3000 Rockfans in der Arena und auf den Rängen des legendären Circus Krone in München, wo die Premiere der ersten Deutschland-Tour von Alice Cooper stattfinden sollte. Ganz vorne vor der Bühne hatte ich mir mit meinen Kameras einen Platz ergattert und war ebenso wie die Fans gespannt auf die Dinge, die da kommen würden.

Als plötzlich mit einem Schlag das Licht ausging, Nebelschwaden aufstiegen, ein einsamer Scheinwerfer über die Bühne huschte und ohne Vorwarnung ein unbeschreiblicher Lärm einsetzte, ahnte das Publikum bereits, dass es sich hier nicht um ein normales Rockkonzert handelte. 45 grellbunte Spots flammten auf, Gitarrengeheul dröhnte jaulend aus den Lautsprechertürmen. Und dann kam der »Frankenstein des Rock« höchstpersönlich auf die Bühne, umgeben von einer Aura aus Horror und Tod. Er sah aus, als wäre er gerade einem Sarg entstiegen: kalkweiß geschminktes Gesicht, blutrote Lippen, schwarz umrandete Augen. Der charismatische Rock-Magier Alice Cooper zog das Publikum von der ersten Sekunde in seinen Bann und entführte es in eine Mischung aus Wunderland und Horrorfilm.

»This is the dark side of me«, drohte Alice zu Beginn des größten Rockspektakels der Welt an, und er hatte nicht zu viel versprochen: Ein Spezial-Effekt jagte den nächsten, Schaufensterpuppen wurden grausam massakriert, die Band inszenierte eine brutale Schlägerei auf der Bühne, Alice kippte eine Mülltonne aus, flirtete mit einer lebendigen Riesenschlange und ging mit dem Hackebeil auf alles los, was sich bewegte. Zu guter Letzt wurde Alice auf dem Elektrischen Stuhl hingerichtet. Aber damit nicht genug – nach seiner »Auferstehung« erhängte er sich selbst mit einem Strick. Das Publikum schrie entsetzt auf. Nebelschwaden verhüllten die grausame Szenerie. Als der Nebel sich verflüchtigte, hing nur noch ein Skelett am Galgen.

Kaum hatte sich das Publikum von diesem Schock erholt, sprang Alice in weißem Frack, Zylinder und glitzernder Paillettenhose auf die Bühne, während Tausende von bunt schillernden Seifenblasen von der Decke schwebten. Nach dem letzten Song »Elected« zerknallte er ein paar Riesenluftballons und sagte grinsend: »Hey! Es war doch alles nur Spaß!«

Das Publikum blieb in einer Mischung aus Ratlosigkeit, Entsetzen, Grauen, Entzücken und Begeisterung zurück. Der Skandal sorgte für Krawall und Aufruhr: So etwas hatte man in München noch nicht gesehen!

DEUTSCHLAND-TOUR 1972

14.11.72	München / Circus Krone
22.11.72	Essen / Gruga-Halle
23.11.72	Hamburg / Musikhalle
24.11.72	Berlin / Deutschlandhalle
25.11.72	Frankfurt / Jahrhunderthalle

ALICE COOPER: SHOCK ROCKER

Summer '72: Alice Cooper released the album »School's Out« in time for the summer holidays, the title track reaching no. 1 in singles charts all over the world. On the last day of school, millions of teenagers worldwide bellowed at the top of their lungs: »Schoooooool's out for summer! Schooooool's out forever!« An anthem had been born.

In October that year, the first warnings spilled across to Germany from the USA: »Watch out – the devil of rock's on his way! Who's afraid of Alice? Who's shaking with fear?«

14 November 1972, Circus Krone in Munich. The show had been sold out for weeks and tickets were changing hands on the black market for astronomical sums. Around 3,000 rock fans had been waiting for an hour, jam-packed into the arena as well as the dress and upper circles of the legendary Circus Krone, where Alice Cooper's German tour was about to open. I'd managed to stake out a space right in front of the stage with my cameras – and was just as excited as everyone else in the venue about what we were shortly to experience.

When the lights abruptly went out, wafts of fog ascended, a single spotlight darted across the stage and a tremendous racket began without warning, the audience realized that what they were about to witness wasn't going to be a run-of-the-mill rock concert. Forty-five gaudily coloured spotlights flared up; the howl of guitars burst out of the loudspeaker stacks. And suddenly the Frankenstein of rock himself appeared on stage, bathed in an aura of horror and death. With his face covered in chalk-white make-up, his blood-red lips and black-edged eyes, he looked as though he'd just climbed out of a coffin. Alice Cooper, the charismatic rock magician, instantly cast a spell over the audience, whisking them off to a place somewhere between Wonderland and a horror movie.

»This is the dark side of me,« threatened Alice at the beginning of the greatest rock spectacle in the world, and he hadn't been exaggerating. One special effect followed the next: display dummies were brutally massacred; the band staged a vicious brawl. Alice knocked a dustbin flying, flirted with a huge live snake and attacked anything that moved with a cleaver. He was executed on the electric chair. And as if that wasn't enough, following his resurrection he hanged himself. The audience screamed in horror. The whole gruesome stage set was enveloped in a dense fog – and when it had disappeared, all that could be seen dangling from the gallows was a skeleton.

Hardly had the audience recovered from the shock when Alice returned onstage dressed in white tails, a top hat and sparkling sequined trousers while thousands of brightly coloured soap bubbles floated down from the ceiling. After the very last song, »Elected,« he burst a couple of massive balloons, grinned and declared: »Hey! I was only joking!«

By this time the audience was in a state of bewilderment, turmoil, horror and delight all rolled into one. Munich had never seen anything like it!

GERMANY TOUR 1972

14.11.72	Munich / Circus Krone
22.11.72	Essen / Gruga-Halle
23.11.72	Hamburg / Musikhalle
24.11.72	Berlin / Deutschlandhalle
25.11.72	Frankfurt / Jahrhunderthalle

EINE SCHLANGE NAMENS YVONNE

»Der einzige Grund für unsere Europa-Tournee war München, wo wir die heißesten Partys feierten. Wir waren alle total verrückt nach dieser Stadt.«

(Alice Cooper in seiner Autobiographie: »Me, Alice«)

Nach der Show im Circus Krone bat uns Alice Cooper zum Interview in seine Suite im 21. Stock des Sheraton Hotels. Meine Reporter-Kollegen Sandro Barretta, K. E. Siegfried und Felix Unruh nahmen Alice ins Kreuzverhör. Zu unserer größten Überraschung war Alice abseits der Bühne ein äußerst freundlicher, witziger und schlagfertiger Gesprächspartner – ein Unterschied wie Dr. Jekyll und Mr. Hyde. Nach dem Interview lud er uns noch zur Aftershow-Party ins »Tiffany's«, damals die heißeste Discothek in München, wo sich VIPs und Stars und natürlich die schönsten Mädchen der Stadt trafen. Sogar Mick Jagger war eines Tages vor einem Stones-Konzert in Innsbruck spontan nach München gedüst, um im Tiffany's zu feiern. Nachdem Mick zunächst mutterseelenallein, fast schüchtern hinter einer Kulisse gestanden und das Treiben beobachtet hatte, hatte ich ihn einfach angequatscht. Er war froh, jemand zu treffen, den er kannte, und fragte mich, ob wir nicht zu mir gehen und ein paar Mädels mitnehmen könnten. Mit drei hübschen Mädchen im Schlepptau landeten wir schließlich an meinem Küchentisch, wo wir bis zum Morgengrauen über Gott, die Welt und Frauen philosophierten.

Auch Alice Cooper schwärmte noch Jahre später in seiner Autobiographie »Me, Alice« über die Aftershow-Party im Tiffany's: »It was like Shangri-La!« – Tatsächlich erinnerte mich diese Party im Tiffany's eher an eine römische Orgie!

15. November 1972
Während der Party hatte ich mich mit Alice Cooper für den nächsten Tag in meinem Fotostudio verabredet. Zu meinem größten Erstaunen erschien Alice einigermaßen pünktlich und halbwegs ausgeschlafen mit seiner Band im Schlepptau, aber zu meinem noch größeren Entsetzen kam er in Begleitung seiner riesigen Würgeschlange!

»Hi Bubi – this is Yvonne! Yvonne – say hello to Bubi!«, sagte er stolz und hängte mir ungefragt die meterlange und etwa 20 Kilo schwere Boa Constrictor um den Hals. Ich weiß nicht, wer von uns beiden darüber mehr entsetzt war, die Schlange oder ich; jedenfalls war ich heilfroh, als Alice seine Begleiterin wieder zurück in ihren Käfig steckte! Später erfuhr ich, dass Alice einmal beinahe von seiner Schlange erdrückt worden wäre und in letzter Sekunde von seinem Leibwächter gerettet werden konnte ...

Neben Yvonne wurde Alice von seinem Freund und Manager Shep Gordon begleitet, der sich während der Fotosession dezent im Hintergrund hielt und sich um Yvonne und die mitgebrachten Requisiten kümmerte. Der Psychologiestudent war der Ideenlieferant für die Show und dachte sich die Gruseleffekte aus. Als Psychologe wusste er natürlich, womit man das Publikum schocken konnte. »Wir spielen ganz bewusst mit den Ängsten und Phobien der Menschen«, erklärte er grinsend. Was mich betraf, hatte er mit Yvonne voll ins Schwarze getroffen!

A SNAKE CALLED YVONNE

»The only reason we went to Europe was so we could have a party in Munich. We were all crazy about this city.«

(Alice Cooper in his autobiography »Me, Alice«)

After the show at Circus Krone, Alice Cooper allowed us to conduct an interview in his suite on the 21st floor of the Sheraton Hotel. He was cross-examined by my fellow reporters Sandro Barretta, K.E. Siegfried and Felix Unruh. To our astonishment, offstage Alice Cooper turned out to be an extremely smart conversationalist who was also very friendly – it was like dealing with Dr Jekyll and Mr Hyde. After the interview, he invited us to the after-show party in Tiffany's, at that time the hottest nightspot in Munich, where VIPs, other celebrities and of course the city's most stunning girls met up.

Even Mick Jagger had on one occasion jetted off to Munich simply in order to go to Tiffany's one day prior to a Rolling Stones show in Innsbruck. After I'd noticed him standing almost shyly in the background with not a soul to talk to, I got chatting to him. He was pleased to see someone he knew and asked if we could take a couple of girls back to my place. With three gorgeous girls in tow, we ended up around my kitchen table philosophizing about God, the world and women until dawn.

Years later, Alice Cooper also went into raptures about the after-show reception at Tiffany's in his autobiography »Me, Alice«: »It was like Shangri-La!« To be honest, I found the party at Tiffany's more reminiscent of a Roman orgy!

15 November 1972
During the party, Alice Cooper had agreed to come to my photo studio the next day. Somewhat surprisingly he arrived with the rest of the band relatively punctually and even seemed to have had a good night's sleep. However, to my horror he had also brought along his giant boa constrictor!

»Hi Bubi – this is Yvonne! Yvonne – say hello to Bubi!« he said proudly, and without so much as a by-your-leave simply plonked the snake, which was about a yard long and easily weighed 40 pounds, around my neck. I wasn't sure who was more terrified: me or the snake! I must say I was thankful and not a little relieved when Alice put Yvonne back into her cage. Later on I learned that Alice had once almost been crushed to death by his snake, only being rescued at the last second by his bodyguard.

Apart from Yvonne, Alice was accompanied by his friend and manager Shep Gordon, who kept out of the way during the photo session and looked after Yvonne and the various props they'd brought with them. A student of psychology, he had provided the ideas for the stage show and thought up the horror effects. Being a psychologist, he knew exactly what buttons to press in order to shock the audience. »We deliberately play with people's fears and phobias,« he explained with a grin. As far as I was concerned, with Yvonne he'd been right on the money!

LIVE IN THE USA:
DIE BILLION-DOLLAR-BABIES-TOUR

»Ich war der größte Act der Welt.«
(Alice Cooper in: »Me, Alice«)

1. März 1973. Rund 20.000 Rockfans waren zur Premiere der US-Tour unter dem Motto »Billion Dollar Babies« in die Convention Center Hall in Detroit gepilgert, die Alice Cooper quer durch ganz Amerika führen und fast eine Million Fans das Gruseln lehren sollte. Ich war exklusiv als einziger Fotograf einer deutschsprachigen Zeitschrift zur Premiere von Alice Coopers neuer Horrorshow eingeladen. Die Bühne war von dem preisgekrönten Designer-Duo Joe Gannon und Jim Newborn entworfen worden und kostete 250.000 US-Dollar. Sie sah aus wie eine gigantische TV-Quiz-Show mit verschiedenen Ebenen und Plattformen. Das Publikum war gespannt: Würde Alice Cooper seine spektakuläre Show überhaupt noch toppen können?

Das erste Lied ertönte: »Hello Hooray«. Alice taumelte auf die Bühne, blieb mit dem Absatz seines silbernen Stiefels hängen, strauchelte, stürzte und sang im Liegen weiter. Das Publikum rätselte: Absicht oder Unfall? Alice sprang plötzlich wieder auf, und dann ging es Schlag auf Schlag: Zuerst wurde er auf einen stählernen OP-Tisch geschnallt und mit einem gigantischen Zahnarztbohrer malträtiert, dann schmuste er mit der Riesenschlange Eva Maria, der Nachfolgerin von Yvonne. Bei »Sick Things« verging er sich an Baby-Puppen und Schaufensterpuppen und riss sie anschließend entzwei. Die Show war an Brutalität kaum noch zu überbieten – ein Leckerbissen für Gruselfans. Das Publikum war sichtlich geschockt. Aber es kam noch besser!

Gemeinsam mit einem Zauberkünstler hatte Alice den grausigen Höhepunkt der Show ausgetüftelt: seine eigene Hinrichtung! Ein Henker packte ihn und zwang ihn vor der drei Meter hohen Guillotine in die Knie. Alice steckte den Kopf in die Öffnung, dann schlossen sich Holzklammern um seinen Hals. Über ihm schwebte das scharfe Messer, das ihn enthaupten sollte. Atemlose Stille. Langsam nahm der Henker den Strick in die Hand, der das Fallbeil auslöste. Alice winkte ein letztes Mal ins Publikum, dann sauste das Messer herunter. Die Menge schrie entsetzt auf. Alices Kopf fiel in einen Korb. Ein Aufschrei ging durch die Halle, als der Henker den blutüberströmten Kopf am Schopf packte und triumphierend hochhielt. Es dauerte eine Weile, bis das Publikum begriff, dass alles nur ein Trick war!

Beim letzten Song »God Bless America« leuchteten Tausende von Wunderkerzen, Alice trug eine riesige US-Flagge und sorgt damit für ein friedliches »Happy End« der Horrorshow.

Wie Alice mir hinterher auf der Aftershow-Party erzählte, war der Trick mit der Guillotine nicht ganz ungefährlich. In dem Augenblick, wo das Fallbeil heruntersauste, musste er blitzschnell seinen Kopf in einen Hohlraum ducken, wo ein Holzklotz das Messer bremste. Alice verriet mir ebenfalls nicht ohne Stolz, dass der abgeschnittene Kopf von dem großen surrealistischen Maler Salvador Dalí entworfen worden war.

Die Party fand auf einem Hotelschiff auf dem Delaware River statt. Auf drei Decks wurde mit Live-Musik, Gauklern, Jongleuren und Künstlern aller Couleur gefeiert. Unter großem Jubel und Applaus wurde Alice Cooper an diesem Abend mit mehreren Goldenen Schallplatten ausgezeichnet. Der Champagner floss in Strömen, so wie vorher das Blut auf der Bühne.

Alices Mutter Ella war auch dabei und sichtlich stolz auf ihren Sprössling, der bestens gelaunt mit seinen Gästen scherzte. Sie erzählte mir, dass ihr Sohn schon immer gerne die Leute zum Lachen gebracht hätte …

LIVE IN THE USA: THE BILLION DOLLAR BABIES TOUR

»I was the biggest act in the world.«
(Alice Cooper in »Me, Alice«)

1 March 1973. About 20,000 rock fans had come to the Convention Center Hall in Detroit to witness the opening night of Alice Cooper's Billion Dollar Babies tour. The tour would take Alice Cooper to virtually every corner of the USA and teach the meaning of fear to almost a million followers. I was the only photographer from a German magazine to be invited to the first night of Alice Cooper's new horror show. The stage set had been designed by the prize-winning designers Joe Gannon and Jim Newborn and had cost $250,000. It was full of platforms at various levels and looked like a giant TV quiz show. The audience was eager to find out whether Alice Cooper would be able to outdo his previous spectacular shows.

Suddenly, the opening number rang out: »Hello Hooray.« Alice staggered on stage, stumbled as the heel of his silver boot got caught, fell over and went on singing lying down. The audience was baffled: was it an accident or just part of the show? All of a sudden, Alice leapt to his feet and the songs came in quick-fire succession. One minute Alice was strapped to a steel operating table and being tortured with a colossal dentist's drill; the next he was canoodling with a giant snake called Eva Maria, Yvonne's successor. During »Sick Things« he began assaulting dolls and showroom dummies before tearing them to pieces. The show's brutality was outrageous – a horror fan's delight! The audience was already visibly shocked – but then Alice went one better.

Alice had teamed up with a conjuror to work out the show's grisly highlight: his own execution! He was grabbed by the executioner, who forced him to his knees in front of a 10-foot-tall guillotine. Alice placed his neck in the lunette, which was then locked to hold him in place. There was a breathless silence. The executioner slowly took hold of the rope to release the blade. Alice waved to the audience for the last time – and the blade came thundering down. The fans gasped in horror as Alice's head fell into a basket; screams rang out as the executioner grabbed the head streaming with blood by the hair and held it up triumphantly. It took a while for the audience to realize it had just been a trick!

During the final song, »God Bless America,« thousands of sparklers were lit. Alice returned bearing a huge Stars and Stripes, bringing his horror show to a happy conclusion.

As Alice revealed to me at the after-show party, the trick with the guillotine was in fact somewhat risky. At the very instant when the blade hurtled towards him, he had to duck his head down into a hollow space where the blade was halted by a block of wood. Alice told me, a touch of pride in his voice, that the head falling off the guillotine had been designed by no less than the great surrealist painter Salvador Dalí.

The party was held on a hotel ship on the Delaware River. The entertainment took the form of live musicians, jugglers and other artists of every description performing on three decks. To great applause, Alice Cooper was awarded a number of gold discs that evening. The champagne flowed – just as the blood had done earlier on stage.

Alice's mother Ella was also at the party and evidently very proud of her boy, who was happily joking with his guests. She confided to me that her son had always enjoyed making people laugh.

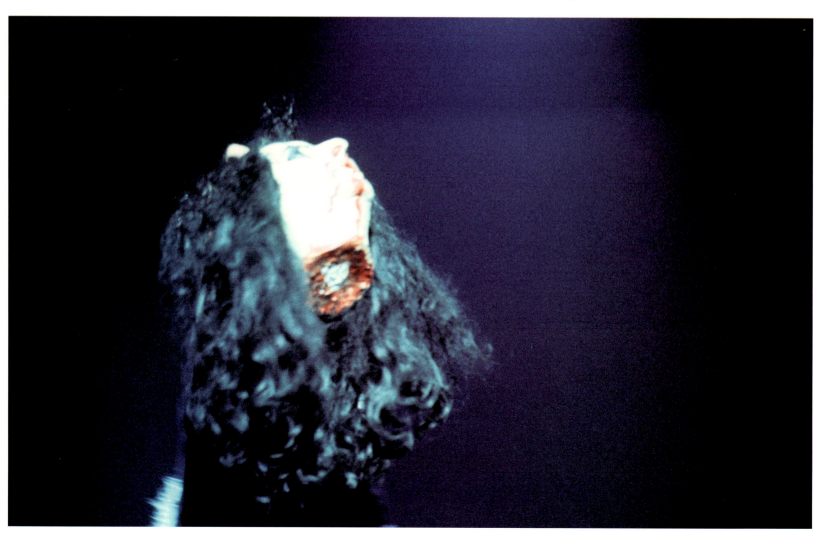

ON TOUR MIT ALICE, USCHI UND DALÍ

Alice lud mich ein, die Band zu den nächsten Gigs der Mammut-Tour durch die USA zu begleiten. Ich durfte im Tourbus mitfahren und in Alice Coopers Privatjet mitfliegen. Dort begegnete ich einer alten Bekannten: Uschi Obermaier, dem Münchner Model, das durch Liaisons mit Mick Jagger und Keith Richards weltberühmt geworden war. Ihr Oben-ohne-Poster hing in Lebensgröße neben Alices Stammplatz. Die echte Uschi wäre ihm wahrscheinlich lieber gewesen …

Bei einer Party in einer Galerie in New York stellte Alice mir sein großes Idol vor: Den exzentrischen spanischen Maler und Künstler Salvador Dalí, der so beeindruckt war von der Alice-Cooper-Show, dass er den Kopf von Alice und dessen Gehirn aus Plastik modelliert hatte. Alice war sichtlich stolz auf seinen berühmten Freund!

Die Billion-Dollar-Babies-Tour brach alle Rekorde und machte ihrem Titel alle Ehre: Die Tour brachte einen Umsatz von 20 Millionen US-Dollar. Auch backstage wurden neue Rekorde aufgestellt: Während der Tour konsumierte die Band 140 Kisten von Alices kanadischem Lieblings-Whiskey Seagrams V.O. sowie sage und schreibe 250.000 (!) Dosen Budweiser Bier! Die Exzesse auf und hinter der Bühne forderten allerdings auch ihren Tribut: Alice war nach der anstrengenden Tour – über 60 Konzerte in 90 Tagen – völlig ausgepowert. Beim letzten Konzert im New Yorker Madison Square Garden schleppte Alice sich mit sechs gebrochenen Rippen und einer Ellbogen-Fraktur auf die Bühne. Die geplante Deutschland-Tour im Anschluss wurde gecancelt. Die umstrittenste Bühnenshow der Welt würden die deutschen Fans also so schnell nicht sehen. Ein paar Monate später erreichte uns aus den USA die schockierende Nachricht: Die Alice-Cooper-Band trennt sich!

Alice & Bubi (Mitte / middle) backstage in Detroit

ON TOUR WITH ALICE, USCHI AND DALÍ

Alice invited me to join the band for the next few gigs on their mammoth tour of the USA. I was allowed to accompany them on the tour bus and even fly on Alice Cooper's private jet. On board I came across an old acquaintance Uschi Obermaier, a Munich model whose affairs with Keith Richards and Mick Jagger had made her worldfamous. Well, it wasn't quite her: it was actually a life-size topless poster of her hanging up next to Alice's seat. No doubt he'd rather have had the real thing!

At a party held in an art gallery in New York, Alice introduced me to his great idol, the eccentric Spanish painter Salvador Dalí, who had been so impressed by Alice Cooper's show that he'd made a plastic model of Alice's head, including the brain. Alice was obviously proud of his famous friend!

The Billion Dollar Babies tour broke all records and almost lived up to its name, the tour revenue reaching $20 million. Records were also broken backstage: during the tour the band drank 140 crates of Alice's favorite whiskey, Canadian Seagrams VO, along with an astonishing 250,000 (!) cans of Budweiser. But the excesses both onstage and backstage took their inevitable toll: following the gruelling tour – 60 concerts in 90 days – Alice was completely washed out. At the last gig in New York's Madison Square Garden, Alice had to drag himself on stage with six broken ribs and a fractured elbow. The German tour scheduled to follow was cancelled, denying German fans the chance to see the most controversial stage show in the world. And a few months later, the news arrived from the USA like a bombshell: Alice Cooper had split.

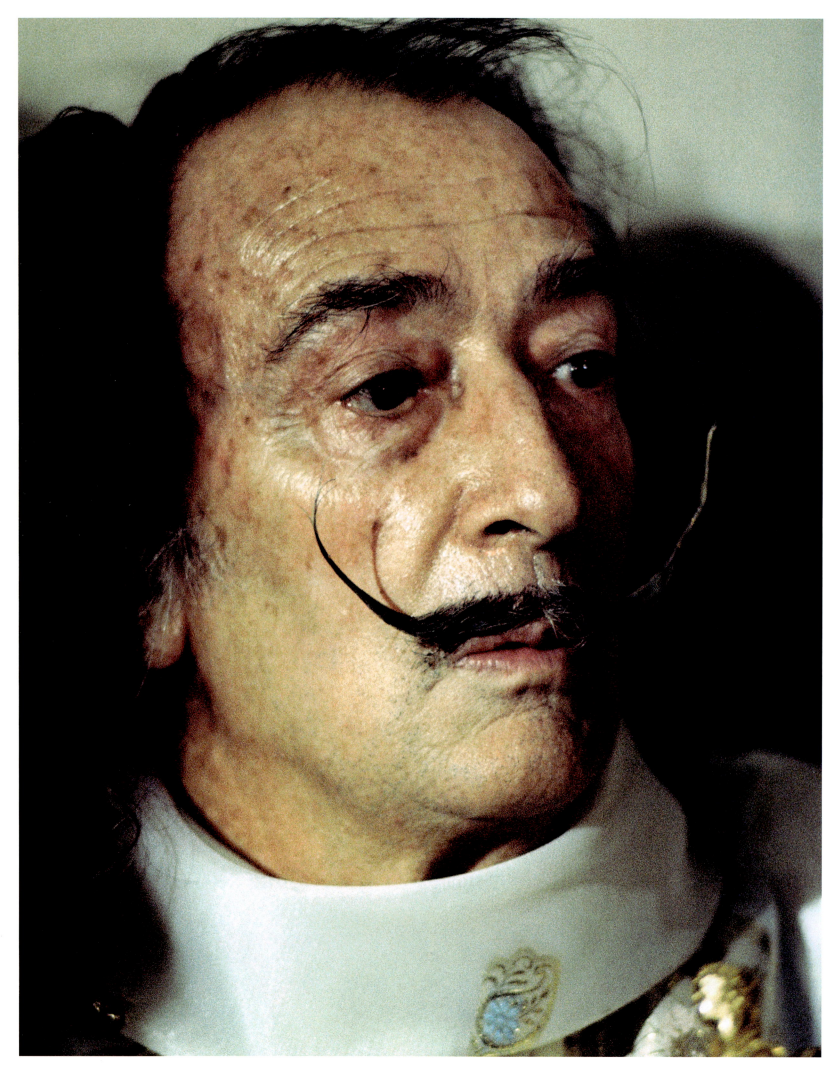

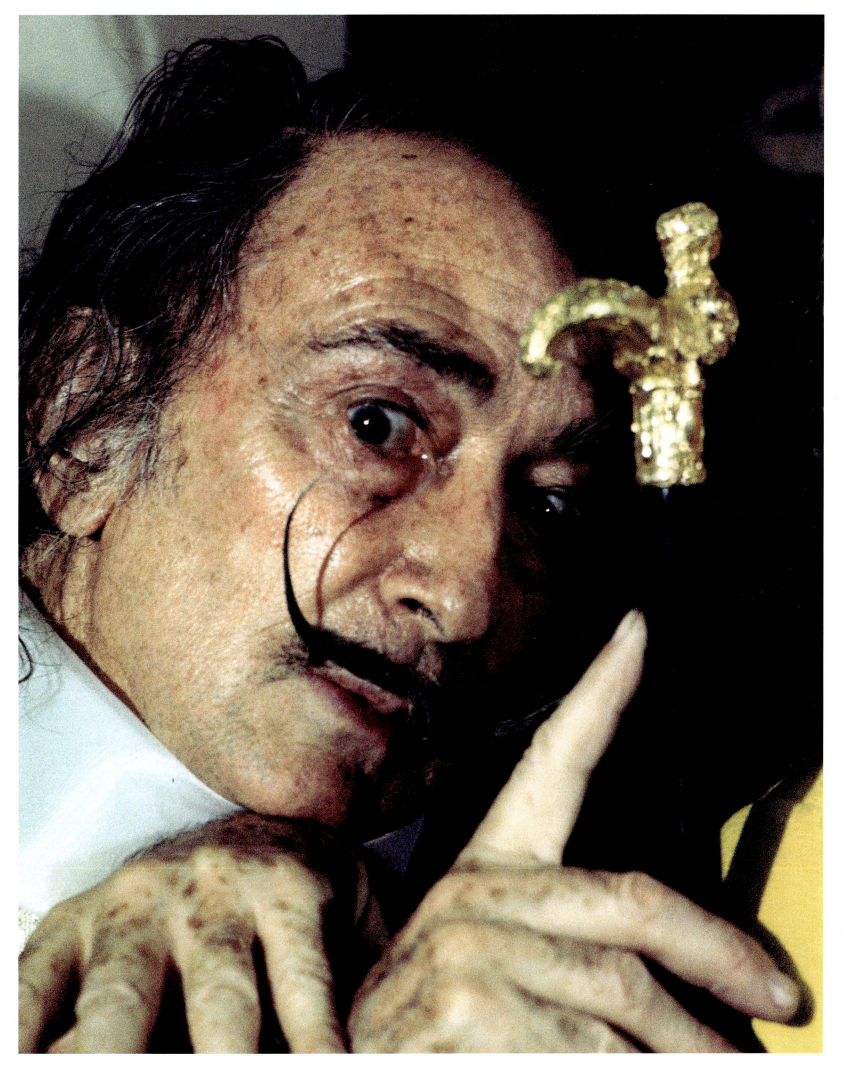

76

77

ALICES ROCKIGE HORROR-SHOW IN DEUTSCHLAND

4. September 1975. Mit einer Stunde Verspätung landete Alice Coopers Privatjet mit der Aufschrift »Alice« um 13 Uhr 58 auf dem Flughafen Bremen zum Start der mehrfach verschobenen Deutschland-Tour. Es war Alice Coopers erster Deutschlandbesuch seit der Trennung von seiner Band.

Die Tür des Fliegers öffnete sich, und Alice erschien auf der Gangway, wie immer gut gelaunt und mit einer Bierdose in der Hand. Als er mich auf dem Rollfeld entdeckte, winkte er fröhlich in die Kamera und kletterte kurzerhand auf einen Polizei-Panzer, der in der Nähe abgestellt war. Alice war total begeistert von diesem Gefährt und fragte mich, wo man so ein Ding kaufen oder mieten konnte. Er wollte unbedingt einen richtigen Panzer in seiner Show haben – koste es, was es wolle! Ich musste ihm schonend beibringen, dass so was in Deutschland unmöglich ist ...

Wir fuhren gemeinsam ins Hotel und verabredeten uns vor dem Konzert an der Bar. Dort am Tresen saß zufällig auch der deutsche Schlagerstar Udo Jürgens. Unterschiedlicher konnten zwei Künstler nicht sein, aber die beiden verstanden sich auf Anhieb! Ich machte sie miteinander bekannt und konnte mir nicht verkneifen, ein Erinnerungsfoto von diesem ungewöhnlichen Paar zu schießen. Einige Udo-Jürgens-Fans, die im Hotel herumlungerten, wollten ihren Augen kaum trauen, als sie ihr Idol mit dem Horrorstar aus den USA an der Bar entdeckten!

Nach einigen Drinks fuhren wir zur Bremer Stadthalle. Über der Halle schwebte, schon von weitem sichtbar, ein riesiger Ballon mit Alices Konterfei.

Ich war gespannt auf die neue Show von Alice Cooper. »Es ist ein völlig neues Konzept«, verriet er mir. Und er hatte nicht zu viel versprochen: Alice verkörperte in der Show einen kleinen Jungen namens Steven, der jede Nacht von schrecklichen Albträumen geplagt wird: Riesenspinnen, überdimensionale Kuscheltiere, die sich in Monster verwandeln, Ratten, Skelette, ein Teddybär, der zu einem Zyklopen mutiert, monströse Fledermäuse, die aus einem schwarzen Sarg flattern und Klein-Steven angreifen. Mit scharfen Säbeln schlug Alice die Riesenmonster in die Flucht und sorgte damit wieder für ein »Happy End«. Die Fans waren von Alice Coopers Nightmare begeistert!

DEUTSCHLAND-TOUR '75:

04.09.75	Bremen
05.09.75	Stuttgart
06.09.75	Ludwigshafen
07.09.75	Wien (Österreich)
08.09.75	München
19.09.75	Hamburg (abgesagt)
20.09.75	Dortmund (abgesagt)

ALICE'S ROCKY HORROR SHOW IN GERMANY

4 September 1975. An hour behind schedule, Alice Cooper's private jet bearing the inscription »Alice« on the hull finally landed at 1.58 pm at Bremen Airport in time to start his postponed German tour. This was Alice Cooper's first trip to Germany since the split.

The aircraft door opened and Alice appeared, in good spirits as always and with a can of beer in his hand. When he saw me on the runway, he waved cheerfully into the camera and without further ado climbed on top of a police tank parked nearby. Alice thought the vehicle was absolutely fantastic and asked me where he could buy or at least hire one. He was determined to have a real tank in his stage show and money was no object! I had to break it to him that that sort of thing was impossible in Germany.

We went to the hotel together and agreed to meet up in the bar before the show. As chance would have it, German superstar Udo Jürgens was also seated at the bar. I introduced them to each other and couldn't resist taking a photograph of this unusual couple! Alice and Udo may have been as different as chalk and cheese, but they got along with each other straight off the bat. A number of Udo Jürgens fans who were hanging around in the hotel couldn't believe their eyes when they saw their idol sharing a drink at the bar with that American horror star!

After a few drinks we set off for the venue in Bremen. A huge hot air balloon with a picture of Alice Cooper that could be seen for miles was hovering above the hall.

I was longing to see what Alice Cooper's new show was like. »It's a totally new concept,« he revealed to me backstage. And this was no exaggeration. During the show, Alice played the role of a little boy called Steven who was plagued by terrible nightmares every night full of giant spiders, outsize cuddly toys that turned into monsters, rats, skeletons, a teddy bear that mutated into a Cyclops, and massive bats which fluttered out of a black coffin to attack him. In the end, Alice drove all the monsters away with his sword to make sure the show had a happy ending. The fans adored Alice's nightmare!

GERMANY TOUR '75:

04.09.75	Bremen
05.09.75	Stuttgart
06.09.75	Ludwigshafen
07.09.75	Vienna (Austria)
08.09.75	Munich
19.09.75	Hamburg (cancelled)
20.09.75	Dortmund (cancelled)

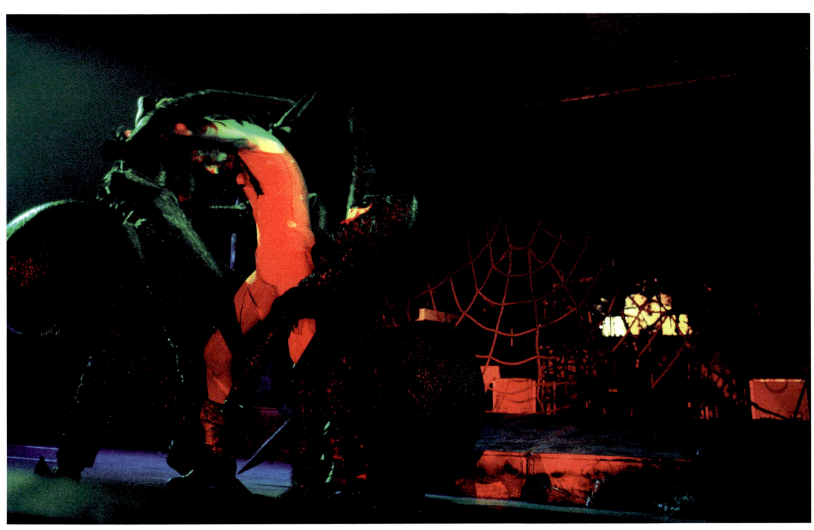

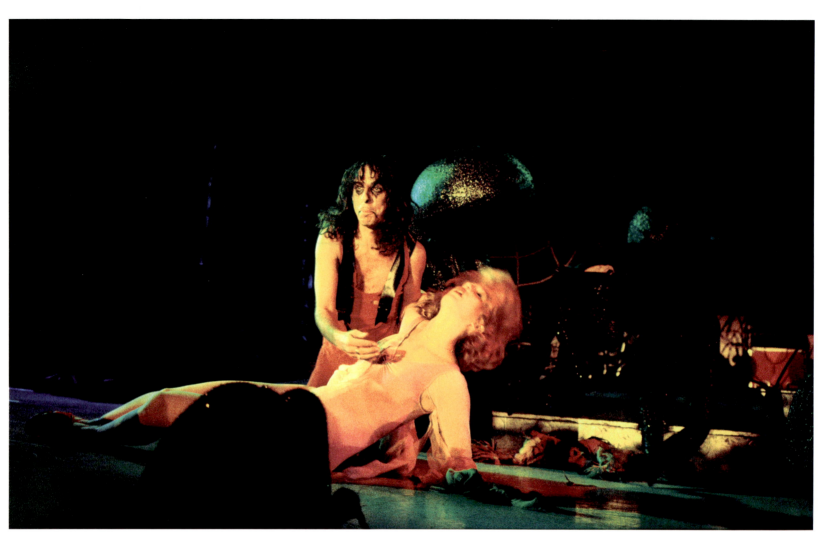

»HI, THIS IS ALICE COOPER SPEAKING!«

8. September 1975. Vier Tage nach dem umjubelten Auftakt zu seiner Deutschland-Tour kam Alice Cooper nach München und besuchte die BRAVO-Redaktion. In einer schwarzen Mercedes-Stretchlimousine 600 Pullmann fuhr er in Begleitung einer seiner Tänzerinnen vor.

Um Alice eine Freude zu machen, hatten wir sein Lebenselixier besorgt: einen Kasten Budweiser. Das brachte ihn natürlich auf Touren! Außerdem hatten wir uns eine kleine Überraschung ausgedacht: Anstelle eines »normalen« Interviews hatten wir die Fans aufgefordert, ihre Fragen für Alice an uns zu schicken. Tausende Briefe und Postkarten hatten daraufhin das Studio überflutet. Alice zog kurzerhand wahllos einige Postkarten aus dem riesigen Stapel und griff höchstpersönlich zum Hörer. Für viele Fans war es ein Schock, als bei ihnen das Telefon klingelte und sich eine Stimme meldete: »Hi! This is Alice Cooper. How are you?«

Geduldig beantwortete Alice sämtliche Fragen und plauderte locker mit seinen Fans. Auf die Frage, ob er sich sportlich betätigte, antwortete er grinsend: »Klar! Ich spiele gemeinsam mit David Cassidy in einem Basketball-Team namens Hollywood Vampires!« Und schließlich entlockte ihm jemand das Geständnis, dass er heimlich für Suzi Quatro schwärmte, seit diese ihn mit ihrer Band als Anheizer auf einer US-Tour begleitet hatte. Aber er betonte: »Ich glaube nicht an Heirat, Unterwäsche und Beerdigungen.« Zum Schluss machte er doch noch eine richtige Liebeserklärung – an München. »Ich liebe München, die Disco Tiffany's, die Mädchen hier, das Bier – und natürlich den Golfplatz Straßlach!« Damals lachten wir alle schallend, aber tatsächlich war Alice Cooper ein leidenschaftlicher Golf-Spieler. Niemand konnte sich vorstellen, wie er in Karohosen und Strickpulli auf dem Fairway die Bälle schlug und ein Wägelchen mit Golfschlägern hinter sich her zog!

Natürlich vergnügte sich Alice Cooper auch in dieser Nacht wieder in seiner Münchner Lieblingsdisco Tiffany's. Doch diesmal gab es ein böses Erwachen. Die Gruppe musste München einen Tag früher verlassen, um bei der Russell Harty Show in England aufzutreten. An dem Morgen wurde die Band stundenlang am Flughafen festgehalten und schikaniert, nachdem sie angeblich ihre Hotelrechnung nicht bezahlt und zudem eine Hotelsuite verwüstet hatten. Daraufhin beschloss die Band, die restlichen zwei Gigs in Deutschland zu canceln und nie wieder deutschen Boden zu betreten. Die Fans waren verzweifelt: Würde Alice Cooper jemals wieder nach Deutschland kommen?

»HI, THIS IS ALICE COOPER SPEAKING!«

8 September 1975. Four days after the acclaimed start to his German tour, Alice Cooper came to Munich to visit BRAVO. He arrived in a black Mercedes 600 Pullman stretch limousine accompanied by one of his dancers.

To make him feel at home, we made sure we had a whole crate of Budweiser lined up – his elixir of life; that soon got him into the swing of things! We'd also come up with a neat little surprise for him: instead of a regular interview, we'd asked fans to write in with questions for Alice. The studio had promptly been inundated with thousands of letters and postcards. Alice picked out a handful of postcards at random from the enormous pile and personally reached for the telephone. Quite a few fans were shocked when the phone rang and the voice at the other end said: »Hi! This is Alice Cooper. How are you?«

Alice patiently answered all the questions and chatted in a relaxed manner with his fans. On being asked whether he did any sport, he grinned and answered: »Sure I do! I play in a basketball team called the Hollywood Vampires together with David Cassidy!« In the end, someone got him to admit that he'd had a secret crush on Suzi Quatro ever since she had been the support act on his US tour. But he went on to stress: »I don't believe in marriage, underwear or funerals!« Finally, he declared that he was head over heels in love – with Munich! »I love Munich, Tiffany's disco, the girls here, the beer – and of course Strasslach golf course!« We all roared with laughter, but in fact by that time Alice Cooper was already a passionate golfer. Nobody could imagine him dressed up in checked trousers and a jumper hitting balls on the fairway and pulling his clubs behind him in a golf cart!

Of course, that night Alice Cooper returned to his favorite nightspot Tiffany's again. But he was in for a nasty shock the next morning. The entire group had to leave Munich a day ahead of schedule in order to appear on the Russell Harty show in the UK. But at the airport they were detained for several hours and harassed because they had supposedly not paid for their hotel room and demolished one of the suites. Furious, the band immediately resolved to cancel their last two gigs in Germany and to never set foot in the country again. His fans were in despair: would Alice Cooper really never return to Germany?

UPDATE

Zunächst schien es, als sei Alice Coopers phänomenale Karriere zu Ende, als er 1976 aus gesundheitlichen Gründen eine US-Tournee kurzfristig absagte und sich eine Erholungspause gönnte. Doch 1977 hatte er mit einer Australien- und der darauf folgenden US-Tournee ein außergewöhnliches Comeback.

Alice Cooper ist ein Phänomen. Ganze Generationen von Musikern hat er inspiriert. Immer wieder wurde er von Kritikern totgesagt, und immer wieder stand er auf wie Phoenix aus der Asche.

2002 gelang ihm erneut ein großes Comeback. Am 2. Dezember 2003 wurde seine Karriere mit einem Stern auf dem berühmten »Walk Of Fame« in Hollywood gekrönt – direkt vor dem Hollywood Roosevelt Hotel, Ecke Hollywood Boulevard und Orange Drive, neben dem Stern von Playboy-Erfinder Hugh Hefner.

Der Meister des schwarzen Humors ist einer der wenigen Künstler, die den Sprung von den wilden Sechzigern und Siebzigern ins neue Jahrtausend geschafft haben, ohne an Anziehungskraft und Popularität zu verlieren. Alice Cooper ist an der Spitze, seit er mit »I'm Eighteen« seinen ersten Hit landete, und es würde mich nicht wundern, wenn er eines Tages mit einer neuen Version unter dem Titel »I'm Eighty« die Charts stürmte ...

Das »Nightmare« ist noch lange nicht zu Ende!

Bubi Heilemann
München, Sommer 2005

UPDATE

At first it seemed that Alice Cooper's extraordinary career was over when he cancelled a US tour in 1976 for health reasons shortly before it opened and took time off to recuperate. But in 1977 he toured first Australia and then the US again, making an extraordinary comeback.

Alice Cooper is a phenomenon. He has inspired entire generations of musicians. Declared finished by the critics on numerous occasions, each time he has arisen again like a phoenix from the ashes.

After yet another comeback in 2002, on 2 December 2003 Alice Cooper received a star on the Hollywood Walk Of Fame for his lifetime achievement. His star is located outside the Hollywood Roosevelt Hotel at the corner of Hollywood Boulevard and Orange Drive, and is next to the star of Playboy founder Hugh Hefner.

The master of black humor is one of the few artists to have managed the transition from the 1960s and 1970s to the new millennium without losing any of his appeal or popularity. Alice Cooper has been at the top of the pile ever since his first hit, »I'm Eighteen,« and I wouldn't be at all surprised to see him back in the charts one day with a slightly revised version entitled »I'm Eighty.«

The nightmare's far from over!

Bubi Heilemann
Munich, Summer 2005

INFORMATIONEN & DANKSAGUNGEN

ALICE COOPER IM INTERNET
www.alicecooper.com (offizielle Webseite)
www.alicecooperstown.com
   (Alice Coopers Restaurant in Phoenix)
www.alicegolf.com (Alice Coopers Golfsite)
www.alicecooper.co.uk (Britische Fansite)
www.palerider.de (Deutsche Fansite)
www.rockfoto.de (Homepage von Bubi Heilemann
   mit Fotos von Alice Cooper u. a.)

CD
Alice Cooper hat mehr als 25 Alben veröffentlicht,
darunter die Compilation »The Life & Crimes of Alice Cooper«
(Rhino Releases CD-Box-Set, Releases from 1969–1997)

DVD
Welcome To my Nightmare (2001)
Brutally Live (2001)
The Ultimate Clip Collection (2003)
Prime Cuts (2003)
Trashes The World (2004)
Roadie (2004)

BÜCHER
»Me, Alice« (Alice Cooper & Steven Gaines)
»Alice Cooper – Welcome To My Nightmare« (Carol Cuellar)
»Billion Dollar Babies« (Bob Greene)

DANKSAGUNG
Besonderer Dank an:
Renate Günther, Sabine Thomas, Herbert Hauke (Rockmuseum München), Thomas Hammerl (Hammerl Communications), Martin Twickler, Wolfgang Krüger.

GANZ HERZLICHEN DANK AN ALICE COOPER!

DIE BUBI HEILEMANN EDITION
Bubi Heilemanns Bücher erscheinen im
Schwarzkopf & Schwarzkopf Verlag.
Bisher sind erschienen:
• ABBA (2004)
• AC/DC (2004)
• BAY CITY ROLLERS (2004),
• ROD STEWART (2005)
Weitere Titel sind in Vorbereitung! Informationen finden Sie
unter www.schwarzkopf-schwarzkopf.de

INFORMATION & ACKNOWLEDGMENTS

ALICE COOPER ON THE INTERNET:
www.alicecooper.com (official website)
www.alicecooperstown.com
   (Alice Cooper's restaurant in Phoenix)
www.alicegolf.com (Alice Cooper's golf website)
www.alicecooper.co.uk (British fansite)
www.palerider.de (German fansite)
www.rockfoto.de (Bubi Heilemann's homepage containing
   photos of Alice Cooper and others)

CDs
Alice Cooper has released more than 25 albums,
including the compilation »The Life & Crimes Of Alice Cooper,«
a Rhino Records box set featuring tracks from 1969 to 1997.

DVDs:
Welcome To My Nightmare (2001)
Brutally Live (2001)
The Ultimate Clip Collection (2003)
Prime Cuts (2003)
Trashes The World (2004)
Roadie (2004)

BOOKS
»Me, Alice« (Alice Cooper & Steven Gaines)
»Alice Cooper – Welcome To My Nightmare« (Carol Cuellar)
»Billion Dollar Babies« (Bob Greene)

ACKNOWLEDGEMENTS:
Special thanks to:
Renate Günther, Sabine Thomas, Herbert Hauke (Rockmuseum Munich), Thomas Hammerl (Hammerl Communications), Martin Twickler, Wolfgang Krüger.

VERY SPECIAL THANKS TO ALICE COOPER!

BUBI HEILEMANN SERIES
The Bubi Heilemann series is published by
Schwarzkopf & Schwarzkopf.
Also published:
• **ABBA (2004)**
• **AC/DC (2004)**
• **BAY CITY ROLLERS (2004)**
• **ROD STEWART (2005)**
Other photographic books are on their way! For more details,
log on to www.soundtrack-distribution.com

BUBI HEILEMANN EDITION

Wolfgang »Bubi« Heilemann war einer der gefragtesten Star-Fotografen der sechziger und siebziger Jahre. Als Exklusiv-Fotograf der damals größten europäischen Jugendzeitschrift BRAVO bekam er alle Superstars dieser schillernden Epoche vor seine Linse. Heilemanns stolze Bilanz: Über 250 BRAVO-Titelbilder, unzählige Poster, Plattencover und natürlich die legendären BRAVO-Starschnitte. In seinem Archiv lagern buchstäblich Millionen von Dias, darunter höchst brisante und bislang unveröffentlichte Aufnahmen von Superstars wie ABBA, AC/DC, Led Zeppelin, Beatles, Rolling Stones, Jimi Hendrix, Bee Gees, Doors, T. Rex, Sweet und vielen anderen Rock-Heroes.

Für die exklusive Bubi-Heilemann-Edition im Verlag Schwarzkopf & Schwarzkopf öffnet Heilemann sein einzigartiges Archiv. Heilemann lässt Bilder lebendig werden und erzählt die Story, die hinter dem Foto steckt. Diese hochkarätige Mischung aus erstklassigem Bildmaterial und fesselnden Storys ist das faszinierende Zeitdokument eines Insiders in Wort und Bild über die größten Superstars der Sixties und Seventies.

1980 hängte Heilemann seine Kamera an den Nagel und wechselte in die Chefredaktion von BRAVO. Später ging er als Regisseur zum Fernsehen, wo er Musiksendungen (BRAVO-TV, FORMEL EINS, TEEN-MAGAZIN) und diverse Features für die ARD drehte. Nebenbei eröffnete er in München Deutschlands ersten Karaoke-Shop.

Heilemanns erster Fotoband »ABBA – Photographien 1974–1980«, erschienen im Frühjahr 2004 in der Edition Bubi Heilemann bei Schwarzkopf & Schwarzkopf, war bereits ein großer Erfolg, ebenso die nachfolgenden Bildbände über AC/DC, die Bay City Rollers und Rod Stewart. Der vorliegende Fotoband über Alice Cooper setzt die erfolgreiche Reihe fort. Weitere Bücher sind bereits in Vorbereitung.

Bubi Heilemanns Ko-Autorin Sabine Thomas wurde bekannt als TV-Moderatorin von Musiksendungen (MUSICBOX, TELE 5 u. a.), Radio-DJane, Musikredakteurin sowie Drehbuch- und Krimi-Autorin.

BUBI HEILEMANN SERIES

Wolfgang »Bubi« Heilemann was one of the most highly acclaimed photographers in the 1960s and 1970s. As the exclusive photographer for what was then Europe's biggest magazine for teenagers, BRAVO, he took pictures of all the superstars who characterized this glittering era. Heilemann's enormous output includes more than 250 front covers, countless posters and record covers, and also the legendary life-size posters of pop stars featured in BRAVO. His archive contains literally millions of unpublished slides, including some highly revealing and previously unseen pictures of superstars such as ABBA, AC/DC, Led Zeppelin, the Beatles, the Rolling Stones, Jimi Hendrix, the Bee Gees, the Doors, T. Rex, Sweet and many other heroes of rock.

Heilemann has now opened up his unique archive for Schwarzkopf & Schwarzkopf's exclusive Bubi Heilemann series. He brings the pictures to life by telling the stories behind them. This exquisite blend of first-class photography and riveting tales is a fascinating contemporary document about the top stars of the sixties and seventies recounted in words and pictures by a genuine insider.

In 1980, Bubi Heilemann retired from photography and became one of the chief editors of BRAVO. Later on he entered the world of television production, making music programs for German TV such as »Bravo-TV,« »Formel Eins« and »Teen-Magazin,« as well as various features. He also opened Germany's first specialist karaoke shop in Munich.

The first book in the series Bubi Heilemann by Schwarzkopf & Schwarzkopf, »ABBA – Photographs 1974–1980,« was published in spring 2004 and was an instant success. It was followed by books featuring photographs of AC/DC, the Bay City Rollers and Rod Stewart. This book on Alice Cooper is the latest addition to this popular series and preparation is already underway for the next few books of photographs.

Bubi Heilemann's co-author Sabine Thomas rose to fame presenting music programs on German TV such as »Musicbox« and »Tele5.« She is also known as a radio deejay, music editor, and a screenplay and crime writer.

Originalfotos können Sie auf
www.rockfoto.de bestellen.

Original photos are available at
www.rockfoto.de.

PHOTOS:
www.rockfoto.de (Homepage of Bubi Heilemann)

Weitere Fotobände in Vorbereitung
Infos unter:
www.schwarzkopf-schwarzkopf.de

Further illustrated books are in preparation
For information please see:
www.soundtrack-distribution.com

Bubi Heilemann
ALICE COOPER
LIVE ON TOUR – BACKSTAGE – PRIVATE
Photos 1973 – 1975
Photos: Wolfgang »Bubi« Heilemann
Text: Bubi Heilemann & Sabine Thomas

ISBN 3-89602-651-8

© der Fotografien: Bubi Heilemann, München 2005 /
 of the photographs: Bubi Heilemann, Munich, 2005
© der Texte: Bubi Heilemann und Sabine Thomas, München
 2005 / of the texts: Bubi Heilemann and Sabine Thomas,
 Munich 2005
© dieser Ausgabe / of this edition:
 Schwarzkopf & Schwarzkopf Verlag GmbH, Berlin 2005

Alle Rechte vorbehalten. Kein Teil dieses Buches darf in irgendeiner Form oder durch elektronische, mechanische oder sonstige Mittel reproduziert werden. Das gilt auch für Archivierungs- und Datenbanksysteme, solange keine schriftliche Genehmigung des Verlages bzw. des Autors vorliegt. Dieses Buch gehört nicht zum offiziellen Alice-Cooper-Merchandising. Jegliche Verwendung der Abbildungen von Bubi Heilemann bedarf seiner ausdrücklichen Genehmigung. Der Verlag vermittelt gern den Kontakt.

All rights reserved. No part of this book may be reproduced in any way or by any electronic, mechanical, or other means. The same applies for archives and databases without previous written permission by the publisher. This book is not part of the Alice Cooper merchandise. Any usage of Bubi Heilemann's pictures must be expressly permitted by the photographer himself. The publisher will be glad to assist in contacting him.

Bildredaktion & Gesamtgestaltung /
 Picture Editing & Layout: Frank Wonneberg
Lektorat / Editor: Linn Schumacher, Anne Litvin
Übersetzung / Translation: Chris Abbey
Retusche & Bildbearbeitung / Retouching &
 Image editing: Radek Polák, Jana Komarkova

KATALOG
Wir senden Ihnen gern kostenlos unseren Katalog.
Bitte schreiben Sie an:
Schwarzkopf & Schwarzkopf Verlag GmbH
Abt. Kundenservice
Kastanienallee 32
D – 10435 Berlin

Telefon: +49 (0) 30 – 44 33 63 00
Fax: + 49 (0) 30 – 44 33 63 044

E-Mail / Internet – for German customers
info@schwarzkopf-schwarzkopf.de
www.schwarzkopf-schwarzkopf.de

E-Mail / Internet – for international customers
info@soundtrack-distribution.com
www.soundtrack-distribution.com